Snail Trail to 100

Sammy Snail's Trail

1	2	3	4	5	6	7	8	9	10
11	12	13	14	15	16	17	18	19	20
21	22	23	24	25	26	27	28	29	30
31	32	33	34	35	36	37	38	39	40
41	42	43	44	45	46	47	48	49	50
51	52	53	54	55	56	57	58	59	60
61	62	63	64	65	66	67	68	69	70
71	72	73	74	75	76	77	78	79	80
81	82	83	84	85	86	87	88	89	90
91	92	93	94	95	96	97	98	99	100

Home

Mr. Bell said to the children,
"Sammy Snail lives at Number 100,
and he has lost his way home.
I want you to make a snail trail
on this chart.

Sammy can stop **five** times on the way.
The trail will show Sammy
how to get home."

3

Mr. Bell read the instructions,
and Joe started to make the snail trail.

On the first day,
Sammy started at number one,
then he went ...

 two spaces to the right

 down one space

Where did Sammy stop on the first day?

Sammy stopped at number 13.

The next day, Sammy went ...

 down one space

 across four spaces to the right

Where did Sammy stop on the second day?

Sammy stopped at number **27**.

On the third day,
Sammy wanted to go a long way.
He went ...

 one space to the right

 down two spaces

 three spaces to the left

Where did Sammy stop on the third day?

Sammy went across to number **28**,
then down to number **48**, then left to number **45**.

On the fourth day,
Sammy didn't go very far.
He went ...

 one space to the left

 down two spaces

Where did Sammy stop on the fourth day?

Sammy went to number **44**.
Then he went down to number **64**.

On the fifth day,
Sammy woke up early.
He went ...

 down one space

 across two spaces to the right

Where did Sammy stop on the fifth day?

Sammy stopped at number **76**.

On the sixth day,
Sammy still had a long way to go.
He had to get home today.
He went ...

 four spaces to the right

 down two spaces

Did Sammy get home?

Yes, Sammy got home,
because he went across to number **80**,
then he went down to number **100**.

Sammy made five stops on his way home. He stopped at ...

13,   27,   45,   64,   76

Sammy Snail's Trail

1	2	3	4	5	6	7	8	9	10
11	12	13	14	15	16	17	18	19	20
21	22	23	24	25	26	27	28	29	30
31	32	33	34	35	36	37	38	39	40
41	42	43	44	45	46	47	48	49	50
51	52	53	54	55	56	57	58	59	60
61	62	63	64	65	66	67	68	69	70
71	72	73	74	75	76	77	78	79	80
81	82	83	84	85	86	87	88	89	90
91	92	93	94	95	96	97	98	99	100

Home

At last, Sammy got home to number 100 on the sixth day.